COLORS OF
PRAYER

AN INTERACTIVE DEVOTIONAL JOURNAL
FOR KIDS

SHILOH  kidz

An Imprint of Barbour Publishing, Inc.

Published by Shiloh Kidz, an imprint of Barbour Publishing, Inc., 1810 Barbour Drive, Uhrichsville, Ohio 44683, www.shilohkidz.com.

Our mission is to inspire the world with the life-changing message of the Bible.

Member of the
Evangelical Christian
Publishers Association

Printed in China.

06567 0819 DS

EXPERIENCE THE POWER OF
PRAYING IN COLOR.

This fun and interactive prayer journal features 7 topics—
each assigned to a vivid color of the rainbow. Quickly
and easily locate a topic that's important to you, read a
faith-building devotion, and then journal your very own
thoughts and prayers. *Colors of Prayer* will help you
talk to God about the things that matter most!

YOUR COLORFUL GUIDE TO PRAYER

SECTION 1

GOD LOVES ME

SEEK, AND YOU WILL FIND

But from there you will look for the Lord your God.
And you will find Him if you look for Him
with all your heart and soul.
DEUTERONOMY 4:29

God loves you. He truly wants a special relationship with you, but He will never force Himself on you. He wants you to desire His presence in your life too. He has promised that if you seek Him with your whole heart, you will find Him. He won't hide in hard places; you just need to go to the right place to discover Him.

Spend some time with God today. Talk to Him in prayer. Talk to Him just like you would your best friend—that *is* what He wants to be, after all. Share your joys with Him. Share your troubles. Let Him experience everything with you. Then choose a passage from the Bible to read, and let God speak to your heart.

Seek Him—you *will* find Him!

God, thank You for always being there just when
I need You. I know You'll never hide from me and that
You truly want to meet with me. . .always. Amen.

*Through faith we understand that
the world was made by the Word of God.*
HEBREWS 11:3

I know that God loves me because he died on the cross so that my sins can be forgiven. He died on the cross for me and my brothers and sisters.

Give me new life because of Your right and good way.
PSALM 119:40

GOD IS RIGHT AND GOOD BECAUSE. . .

Jesus looked at them and said, "This cannot be done by men. But with God all things can be done."
MATTHEW 19:26

DO YOU TALK TO GOD MORE WHEN YOU'RE HAVING A HARD TIME?

Let the wise man. . .think about the
loving-kindness of the Lord.
PSALM 107:43

WHEN YOU'RE GOING THROUGH A DIFFICULT TIME,
DO YOU TALK TO GOD FIRST—BEFORE ANYONE ELSE?

Be right with [God]. All these other
things will be given to you also.
MATTHEW 6:33

WHY WILL GOD ALWAYS GUIDE YOU IN THE RIGHT DIRECTION?

If you do not have wisdom, ask God for it. He is always ready to give it to you and will never say you are wrong for asking.
JAMES 1:5

WHAT ARE YOU ASKING GOD FOR TODAY?

I will show you and teach you in the way you should go.
I will tell you what to do with My eye upon you.
PSALM 32:8

DO YOU HAVE A FAVORITE SCRIPTURE? WHY IS IT YOUR FAVORITE?

Have joy in His holy name. Let the heart of those who look to the Lord be glad.
1 CHRONICLES 16:10

DOES KNOWING GOD MAKE YOUR HEART GLAD?

How much more will your Father in heaven
give good things to those who ask Him?
MATTHEW 7:11

WHAT GOOD THINGS HAS GOD GIVEN YOU?

Trust in the Lord with all your heart, and do not trust in your own understanding. Agree with Him in all your ways, and He will make your paths straight.
PROVERBS 3:5-6

IS THERE SOMEONE IN YOUR LIFE WHO NEEDS TO KNOW GOD? HOW CAN YOU PRAY FOR HIM OR HER?

How happy is the man whose strength is in You.
PSALM 84:5

WHAT THINGS REMIND YOU OF GOD'S LOVE?

This book of the Law must not leave your mouth.
Think about it day and night, so you may be careful
to do all that is written in it. Then all will go well
with you. You will receive many good things.
JOSHUA 1:8

DO YOU THINK IT'S IMPORTANT TO MEMORIZE SCRIPTURE? WHY OR WHY NOT?

Do your best to know that God is pleased with you.
Be as a workman who has nothing to be ashamed of.
Teach the words of truth in the right way.
2 TIMOTHY 2:15

DO YOU PRAY FOR GOD TO DO WHAT'S BEST FOR YOUR
LIFE? OR DO YOU USUALLY WANT THINGS YOUR OWN WAY?

This is the reason I have sent him to you. It is so you can know about us. He can also bring joy to your hearts.
COLOSSIANS 4:8

Section 2

GOD WANTS ME TO GROW CLOSER TO HIM

A SPECIAL MESSAGE

---

*When they read it, they were glad for
the comfort and strength it brought them.*
Acts 15:31

Are you happy, sad, excited, or disappointed? Celebrating or feeling down? . . . Lonely, loved, worried, nervous? . . . No matter what you're feeling, God's Word *always* has a message for you—a message that will help you with anything and everything you care about, whatever's on your mind. Your life is important to the One who created you!

So pick up your Bible and get reading! Set aside a special time of day to spend with the One who loves you more than anyone or anything. Highlight, underline, or circle the passages that speak to your heart.

When you're through spending time in God's Word, you'll have time to reflect and write in a journal. And the best part? . . . You'll find yourself growing closer to the heavenly Father *every day*!

---

*God, please help me to stay faithful, spending
time in Your Word every day. Thank You! Amen.*

Jesus said to them, "For sure, I tell you this: If you have faith and do not doubt, you will not only be able to do what was done to the fig tree. You will also be able to say to this mountain, 'Move from here and be thrown into the sea,' and it will be done. All things you ask for in prayer, you will receive if you have faith."
MATTHEW 21:21-22

DO YOU BELIEVE THAT GOD WILL
ALWAYS ANSWER WHEN YOU PRAY?

In this way, you do not have faith in Christ because of the wisdom of men. You have faith in Christ because of the power of God.
1 CORINTHIANS 2:5

HAVE YOU EVER WONDERED WHY GOD WAS
TAKING SO LONG TO ANSWER YOUR PRAYER?

Watch and keep awake! Stand true to the Lord.
Keep on acting like men and be strong.
1 CORINTHIANS 16:13

IS IT HARD FOR YOU TO BE PATIENT
WHILE WAITING FOR GOD TO ANSWER?

Wait for the Lord. Be strong. Let your
heart be strong. Yes, wait for the Lord.
PSALM 27:14

DO YOU TRUST THAT GOD WILL GIVE YOU JUST
WHAT YOU NEED—AND AT THE RIGHT TIME?

*If we tell Him our sins, He is faithful and we
can depend on Him to forgive us of our sins.
He will make our lives clean from all sin.*
1 JOHN 1:9

DO YOU HAVE A FAVORITE SCRIPTURE THAT REMINDS YOU TO SPEND TIME WITH GOD?

You have never seen Him but you love Him. You cannot see Him now but you are putting your trust in Him. And you have joy so great that words cannot tell about it.
1 PETER 1:8

HOW DOES IT FEEL TO KNOW THAT
YOU CAN TALK TO GOD ABOUT ANYTHING?

Do not worry. Learn to pray about everything. Give thanks to God as you ask Him for what you need. The peace of God is much greater than the human mind can understand. This peace will keep your hearts and minds through Christ Jesus.
PHILIPPIANS 4:6–7

HOW DO YOU FEEL AFTER YOU'VE HAD A TALK WITH GOD?

You will show me the way of life. Being with You is to be full of joy. In Your right hand there is happiness forever.
PSALM 16:11

WHEN WAS THE LAST TIME YOU TALKED TO GOD?
WAS IT THIS MORNING? . . . LAST NIGHT? . . .
LAST WEEK? . . . LAST MONTH?

Give all your cares to the Lord and He will give you strength.
He will never let those who are right with Him be shaken.
PSALM 55:22

WHAT HARD THING DO YOU NEED
TO SHARE WITH GOD TODAY?

See! I stand at the door and knock. If anyone hears My voice and opens the door, I will come in to him and we will eat together.
REVELATION 3:20

HOW DOES IT FEEL TO KNOW THAT GOD DOESN'T
MISS ONE SINGLE WORD WHEN YOU TALK TO HIM?

See what great love the Father has for us that He would call us His children. And that is what we are. For this reason the people of the world do not know who we are because they did not know Him.
1 JOHN 3:1

DO YOUR WORRIES EVER DISTRACT
YOU FROM SPENDING TIME WITH GOD?

*"Come to Me, all of you who work and
have heavy loads. I will give you rest."*
MATTHEW 11:28

DOES PRAYER EVER HELP YOUR
BAD FEELINGS TURN TO GOOD?

The Lord your God is with you, a Powerful One Who wins the battle. He will have much joy over you. With His love He will give you new life. He will have joy over you with loud singing.
ZEPHANIAH 3:17

WHEN DO YOU FEEL LIKE GOD IS CLOSEST TO YOU?

*Let the words of my mouth and the thoughts
of my heart be pleasing in Your eyes, O Lord,
my Rock and the One Who saves me.*
PSALM 19:14

DO YOU SET ASIDE TIME EACH DAY FOR ONE-ON-ONE TIME WITH GOD?

Of what great worth is Your loving-kindness,
O God! The children of men come and
are safe in the shadow of Your wings.
PSALM 36:7

HOW IMPORTANT IS PRAYER TO YOU?

Those who are right with the Lord cry, and He hears them.
And He takes them from all their troubles.
PSALM 34:17

SECTION 3

GOD WANTS ME TO HAVE A THANKFUL HEART

EVERYTHING THAT'S GOOD!

Always give thanks for all things to God the Father in the name of our Lord Jesus Christ.
EPHESIANS 5:20

Bad days? We all have them. And you've been there with. . .the haircut that didn't turn out like you wanted, the reprimand from your teacher for talking in class, the less-than-perfect grade on your spelling test, and the bruised knees from your embarrassing trip over your chair in Sunday school.

We can't always control things that go wrong, but what we can control is our reaction to those things. So the next time you have a bad day, think about the wonderful things in your life—like your wonderful family, your cuddly pet, your best friend, your bedroom that's decorated just the way you like it—and you'll find yourself bouncing back fast from your sour mood.

And last but not least, thank God for all the good stuff in your life. He'll be happy to hear from you!

God, when things don't quite go my way, instead of feeling sorry for myself, help me to think of everything that's good—there are a lot of wonderful things in this life of mine! Thank You for blessing me! Amen.

*Go into His gates giving thanks and into His holy place
with praise. Give thanks to Him. Honor His name.*
PSALM 100:4

WHAT IS THE LAST THING YOU THANKED GOD FOR?

I will praise the name of God with song.
And I will give Him great honor with much thanks.
PSALM 69:30

IS IT DIFFICULT TO BE THANKFUL DURING HARD TIMES?

Praise the Lord, O my soul. And all
that is within me, praise His holy name.
PSALM 103:1

ISN'T IT WONDERFUL THAT GOD LOVES
AND ACCEPTS YOU NO MATTER WHAT?
THANK HIM RIGHT NOW!

A man cannot please God unless he has faith.
Anyone who comes to God must believe that He is.
That one must also know that God gives what is
promised to the one who keeps on looking for Him.
HEBREWS 11:6

WHAT ARE YOU MOST THANKFUL FOR TODAY?

In everything give thanks. This is what
God wants you to do because of Christ Jesus.
1 Thessalonians 5:18

TODAY, BE THANKFUL THAT YOU NEVER HAVE
TO GO THROUGH SOMETHING HARD ALONE.

HOW DOES THAT MAKE YOU FEEL?

Praise the Lord! How happy is the man who honors the Lord with fear and finds joy in His Law!
PSALM 112:1

GOD TAKES GREAT DELIGHT IN YOU.
DO YOU DELIGHT IN HIM AS WELL?

Good will come to the man who trusts in the Lord, and whose hope is in the Lord.

JEREMIAH 17:7

DO YOU TRUST THAT GOD WILL ALWAYS DO WHAT'S BEST FOR YOU?

Jesus said to him, "Why are you asking Me about what is good? There is only One Who is good. If you want to have life that lasts forever, you must obey the Laws."
MATTHEW 19:17

WHAT IS YOUR FAVORITE SCRIPTURE THAT REMINDS YOU TO ALWAYS HAVE A THANKFUL HEART?

How great is Your loving-kindness! You have stored it up for those who fear You. You show it to those who trust in You in front of the sons of men.
PSALM 31:19

HOW HAS GOD BLESSED YOU?

In the beginning God made from nothing the heavens and the earth.
GENESIS 1:1

WHAT DO YOU ENJOY MOST ABOUT GOD'S CREATION? THANK HIM TODAY.

You get what is coming to you when you sin.
It is death! But God's free gift is life that lasts
forever. It is given to us by our Lord Jesus Christ.
ROMANS 6:23

IF YOU HAVE ACCEPTED GOD'S GIFT OF
SALVATION, YOU WILL LIVE FOREVER IN HEAVEN.
THINK ABOUT THAT. . .AND GIVE THANKS!

The loving-kindness of God lasts all day long.
PSALM 52:1

YOUR HEAVENLY FATHER IS A GOD WHO GIVES
SECOND CHANCES WHEN YOU MAKE A MISTAKE.
HOW HAS HE OFFERED YOU A SECOND CHANCE?

Because of the blood of Christ, we are bought and made free from the punishment of sin. And because of His blood, our sins are forgiven. His loving-favor to us is so rich. He was so willing to give all of this to us. He did this with wisdom and understanding.

EPHESIANS 1:7–8

THINK ABOUT THE LAST TIME YOU FELT SO VERY THANKFUL.
DID YOU REMEMBER TO SAY "THANK YOU" TO GOD?

Be full of joy all the time. Never stop praying.
1 THESSALONIANS 5:16–17

YOU DON'T HAVE TO FIND GOD.
HE HAS ALREADY FOUND YOU.
DOESN'T THAT MAKE YOUR HEART THANKFUL?

All the paths of the Lord are loving and true for those who keep His agreement and keep His Laws.
PSALM 25:10

WHEN YOU LAST TALKED TO GOD, DID YOU TELL HIM "THANK YOU" FOR ALL HE'S DONE FOR YOU?

Sing to Him. Sing praises to Him.
Tell of all His great works.
1 CHRONICLES 16:9

SECTION 4
GOD GIVES ME HOPE

A SPECIAL KIND OF HOPE

Love each other. . . . Show respect for each other. Do not be lazy but always work hard. Work for the Lord with a heart full of love for Him. Be happy in your hope. Do not give up when trouble comes. Do not let anything stop you from praying. Share what you have with [those] who are in need. Give meals and a place to stay to those who need it.
ROMANS 12:10–13

There is a recipe for success in these scriptures—a recipe for success in the Christian life. God doesn't give us instruction just to boss us around. He knows that if we can stick to this "recipe," we will be the kind of Christians He calls us to be.

One ingredient mentioned in these verses is hope. Not just any hope, but *confident* hope. There is a difference between plain hope and *confident* hope. You can hope the wind doesn't blow today, but you don't know for sure that it won't. You can hope those shoes you've been wanting will go on sale, but there is no guarantee they will. *Confident* hope is a sure thing. . .like the hope of God's love and a future home in heaven. These things are guaranteed if we have chosen to follow Jesus. We can have this kind of hope all the time. It's a special gift—a gift that God gives to us as a promise.

Aren't you happy to have God's special kind of hope?

Dear Lord, thank You for the gift of hope. Help me to share it with others and show them by the way I live that I have the perfect recipe for life. I will rejoice in the hope You have given me. Amen.

HOW CAN TIME IN GOD'S WORD IMPROVE YOUR MOOD?

He heals those who have a broken heart.
He heals their sorrows.
PSALM 147:3

HOW DOES THE HEAVENLY FATHER HELP YOU MAKE THE BEST OF A BAD SITUATION?

And now, Lord, what do I wait for?
My hope is in You.
PSALM 39:7

WHEN YOU ARE SAD, DO YOU TRUST THAT
GOD WILL TURN THINGS RIGHT-SIDE UP?

*Why are you sad, O my soul? Why have you
become troubled within me? Hope in God,
for I will praise Him again, my help and my God.*
PSALM 43:5

WHAT COMFORTS YOU MOST DURING HARD TIMES?

This hope is a safe anchor for our souls.
It will never move.
HEBREWS 6:19

WHAT WORRIES YOU MOST?
GIVE IT TO GOD, THE HOPE GIVER, TODAY.

My soul becomes weak with desire for Your saving power, but I have put my hope in Your Word.
PSALM 119:81

WHAT IS A FAVORITE SCRIPTURE THAT CALMS YOUR WORRIES?

*But as for me, I will always have hope
and I will praise You more and more.*
PSALM 71:14

THINK ABOUT THE MIRACLES OF THE BIBLE.
HAVE YOU EVER SEEN A MIRACLE IN YOUR OWN LIFE?

If I take the wings of the morning or live in the farthest part of the sea, even there Your hand will lead me and Your right hand will hold me.
PSALM 139:9–10

WHAT DO YOU IMAGINE HEAVEN WILL BE LIKE?

*"Do not be sad for the joy of
the Lord is your strength."*
NEHEMIAH 8:10

DO YOU EVER FEEL LIKE NO ONE REALLY
LISTENS TO OR UNDERSTANDS YOU?

HOW DOES IT FEEL TO KNOW THAT YOU HAVE
A HEAVENLY FATHER WHO DOESN'T MISS A WORD AND
WHO UNDERSTANDS YOU LIKE NO ONE ELSE EVER COULD?

*I rise before the morning comes and cry
for help. I have put my hope in Your Word.*
PSALM 119:147

DOES TALKING TO GOD HELP YOU TO HAVE HOPE?

For if a man belongs to Christ, he is a new person.
The old life is gone. New life has begun.
2 CORINTHIANS 5:17

ARE YOU TIRED AND TROUBLED?
ASK GOD TO GIVE YOU HIS COMFORT AND PEACE.

My soul is quiet and waits for God alone.
My hope comes from Him.
PSALM 62:5

DO YOU FEEL CLOSE TO GOD TODAY?
WHY OR WHY NOT?

"[God] is not far from each one of us."
ACTS 17:27

WHAT ARE YOU HOPING FOR TODAY?

Now faith is being sure we will get what we hope for. It is being sure of what we cannot see.
HEBREWS 11:1

DO YOU HAVE FAITH IN GOD EVEN
THOUGH YOU CAN'T SEE HIM?

I pray that your hearts will be able to understand.
I pray that you will know about the hope given by
God's call. I pray that you will see how great the things
are that He has promised to those who belong to Him.
EPHESIANS 1:18

DO YOU KNOW SOMEONE WHO NEEDS GOD'S COMFORT?
PRAY FOR THAT PERSON RIGHT NOW.

I can do all things because
Christ gives me the strength.
PHILIPPIANS 4:13

SECTION 5

GOD FORGIVES (AND HE WANTS ME TO FORGIVE TOO!)

FORGIVENESS

But God showed His love to us.
While we were still sinners, Christ died for us.
ROMANS 5:8

One of the greatest things about God is that He knows all our flaws, and yet He loves us unconditionally. Yep, God loves you when you mess up or make a mistake. And there is nothing—*absolutely nothing!*—you can do to cause Him to stop loving you.

The Bible says that God sent His Son, Jesus, to die for us *while we were still sinners*. He didn't wait for us to clean up our act. He sent Jesus to pay the price for our sins. He knows us, and He loves us just the way we are.

Think about the grace that God pours out on you as He forgives your sins. Do you show grace to other people when they make mistakes? One way that others can see God in you is through forgiveness. Choose to forgive today!

God, thank You for Your forgiveness.
Help me to be forgiving. Amen.

"I am all you need. I give you My loving-favor. My power works best in weak people." I am happy to be weak and have troubles so I can have Christ's power in me.
2 Corinthians 12:9

IS IT POSSIBLE TO BE HAPPY EVEN IN HARD TIMES? WHY OR WHY NOT?

*"I will show loving-kindness to them and forgive
their sins. I will remember their sins no more."*
HEBREWS 8:12

HOW DOES IT FEEL TO KNOW THAT
GOD LOOKS ON YOU WITH HOLY FAVOR?

You must be kind to each other. Think of the other person. Forgive other people just as God forgave you because of Christ's death on the cross.
EPHESIANS 4:32

IS IT DIFFICULT TO FORGIVE SOMEONE WHO HAS HURT YOU? WHY OR WHY NOT?

I came so they might have life, a great full life.
JOHN 10:10

WHY IS IT IMPORTANT TO FORGIVE OTHERS?

*Those who belong to Christ will
not suffer the punishment of sin.*
ROMANS 8:1

WHEN YOU TALK TO GOD, IS IT HARD FOR YOU
TO SHARE EVERYTHING THAT'S ON YOUR MIND?

He will again have loving-pity on us. He will crush our sins under foot. Yes, You will throw all our sins into the deep sea.
MICAH 7:19

GOD WILL ALWAYS GIVE YOU A BRAND-NEW START.
ASK HIM TODAY!

Try to understand other people. Forgive each other.
If you have something against someone, forgive him.
That is the way the Lord forgave you.
COLOSSIANS 3:13

IS THERE SOMEONE YOU NEED TO FORGIVE TODAY?

*Forgive other people and other
people will forgive you.*
LUKE 6:37

IS THERE SOMEONE YOU NEED TO APOLOGIZE TO TODAY?

*If My people who are called by My name put away
their pride and pray, and look for My face, and turn
from their sinful ways, then I will hear from heaven.
I will forgive their sin, and will heal their land.*
2 CHRONICLES 7:14

IF SOMEONE HAS HURT YOUR FEELINGS,
IS IT HARD FOR YOU TO TALK ABOUT IT?

Is anyone among you suffering? He should pray. Is anyone happy? He should sing songs of thanks to God.
JAMES 5:13

IS THERE SOMEONE YOU HAVE RECENTLY WRONGED? WHAT CAN YOU DO TO MAKE IT RIGHT?

Do not let kindness and truth leave you. Tie them around your neck. Write them upon your heart.
PROVERBS 3:3

WHEN OTHERS LOOK AT YOU, WHAT DO THEY SEE?
DO THEY SEE A HEART FULL OF GOODNESS,
GENTLENESS, AND LOVE?

*Make a clean heart in me, O God. Give
me a new spirit that will not be moved.*
PSALM 51:10

WHEN YOU SIN, INSTEAD OF ANGER,
GOD EXTENDS HIS LOVE AND GRACE.
HOW DOES THAT MAKE YOU FEEL?

*"You will know the truth and
the truth will make you free."*
JOHN 8:32

NO MATTER HOW "BIG" YOUR SIN IS,
GOD WILL FORGIVE YOU.

HOW DOES IT FEEL TO KNOW THAT HE DOESN'T MEASURE
YOUR SIN BEFORE HE OFFERS HIS LOVING GRACE?

For the good of Your name, O Lord,
forgive my sin, even as big as it is.
PSALM 25:11

WHAT IS YOUR FAVORITE SCRIPTURE ABOUT FORGIVENESS?

God has chosen you. You are holy and loved by Him. Because of this, your new life should be full of loving-pity. You should be kind to others and have no pride. Be gentle and be willing to wait for others.
Colossians 3:12

DO YOU TRUST, WITHOUT A DOUBT, THAT GOD
WILL FORGIVE ANY AND ALL OF YOUR SINS?
WHY OR WHY NOT?

*How happy he is whose wrong-doing
is forgiven, and whose sin is covered!*
PSALM 32:1

SECTION 6

GOD WANTS ME TO PRAY FOR MY FAMILY AND FRIENDS

INVITE GOD

"For where two or three are gathered together in My name, there I am with them."
Matthew 18:20

You probably know people who are always ready for a party. They're the ones who make their way to every gathering and are always ready to hang out with anyone and everyone. Social by nature, they enjoy spending time with people and cannot wait for an invitation so they can mingle with others.

God's the same way. He yearns for the time when two or three people gather together to pray, study His Word, offer help to others, or simply spend time together in Christian friendship; and then the Holy Spirit shows up, just like that. He arrives for the smallest of meetings and the biggest of corporate worship services—they're all important to Him.

The next time you seek the presence of your heavenly Father, meet with a friend or family member or two and invite God to join you. He'll be there even before you ask.

*God, thank You for showing up whenever I ask. . .
before I even ask. I am so thankful that what matters
to me also matters very much to You. Amen.*

A friend loves at all times.
A brother is born to share troubles.
PROVERBS 17:17

HOW DOES IT MAKE YOU FEEL WHEN A FRIEND OR FAMILY MEMBER IS HAVING A HARD TIME? WHAT CAN YOU DO TO HELP?

The man who is right with God is a teacher to his neighbor,
but the way of the sinful leads them the wrong way.

WHY ARE RELATIONSHIPS SO IMPORTANT?

He who covers a sin looks for love. He who tells of trouble separates good friends.
PROVERBS 17:9

WHAT CAN YOU DO TO HELP IMPROVE YOUR RELATIONSHIPS WITH FAMILY AND FRIENDS?

If we love each other, God lives in us.
His love is made perfect in us.
1 JOHN 4:12

DID YOU KNOW THAT YOU ARE PART OF GOD'S FAMILY?

Fervently love one another from the heart.
1 Peter 1:22 NASB

WHICH RELATIONSHIPS DO YOU CHERISH MOST?
WHY?

You have made your souls pure by obeying the truth through the Holy Spirit. This has given you a true love for the Christians. Let it be a true love from the heart.
1 Peter 1:22

DO YOU HAVE FRIENDS OR FAMILY
MEMBERS WHO DON'T KNOW GOD?
SAY A PRAYER FOR THEM NOW.

Two are better than one, because they have good pay for their work. For if one of them falls, the other can help him up. But it is hard for the one who falls when there is no one to lift him up.
ECCLESIASTES 4:9–10

WHAT IS A FAVORITE MEMORY YOU HAVE OF A FRIEND OR FAMILY MEMBER? THANK GOD FOR THE BLESSING OF MEMORY TODAY!

A heart that has peace is life to the body, but wrong desires are like the wasting away of the bones.
PROVERBS 14:30

WHEN WAS THE LAST TIME YOU HAD A DISAGREEMENT WITH A FRIEND? HOW DID YOU HANDLE IT?

DO YOU TELL YOUR FRIENDS AND FAMILY
HOW MUCH YOU LOVE THEM?

DO YOU *SHOW* THEM THROUGH YOUR ACTIONS AS WELL?

*We should do good to everyone. For sure,
we should do good to those who belong to Christ.*
GALATIANS 6:10

HOW CAN YOU HELP YOUR FRIENDS AND FAMILY GROW IN THEIR RELATIONSHIP WITH GOD?

"Kindness from a friend should be shown to a man without hope, or he might turn away from the fear of the All-powerful."
JOB 6:14

DO YOU HAVE FRIENDS OR FAMILY WHO MIGHT NEED A CARING WORD FROM YOU TODAY?

*Last of all, you must share the same thoughts
and the same feelings. Love each other with a
kind heart and with a mind that has no pride.*
1 PETER 3:8

IN WHAT WAYS CAN YOU HONOR GOD IN YOUR RELATIONSHIPS?

Keep your minds thinking about whatever is true, whatever is respected, whatever is right, whatever is pure, whatever can be loved, and whatever is well thought of. If there is anything good and worth giving thanks for, think about these things.
PHILIPPIANS 4:8

HAVE YOU SAID A PRAYER OF THANKS FOR ALL OF THE RELATIONSHIPS WITH WHICH GOD HAS BLESSED YOU?

"Do for other people whatever you would like to have them do for you. This is what the Jewish Law and the early preachers said."
MATTHEW 7:12

DO YOU EVER GET ANGRY OR FRUSTRATED WITH A FRIEND OR FAMILY MEMBER? HOW COULD YOU HANDLE YOUR EMOTIONS BETTER DURING THOSE TIMES?

Think as Christ Jesus thought.
PHILIPPIANS 2:5

WHY DO YOU THINK GOD CREATED HUMANS TO HAVE RELATIONSHIPS WITH ONE ANOTHER?

"But as for me and my family, we will serve the Lord."
JOSHUA 24:15

SECTION 7

GOD HAS A PLAN FOR MY FUTURE

FATHER KNOWS BEST

Your Father knows what you need before you ask Him.
MATTHEW 6:8

"But I prayed about it! Why didn't it work out?"

If you've ever asked this question, then you know how disappointing it is when your prayers seem to go unanswered. No matter how many promises and miracles there are in the Bible, the one you're looking for is the most important. And if it doesn't show up, you might find yourself wondering if there really is a God who listens and cares.

Rest assured that God hears His children each and every time they call. But like all good parents, your heavenly Father decides whether your petition is a good one. Some answers to prayer are delayed until the timing is right. Other prayers are denied because they don't fit into God's plan for your life. And sometimes God thrills your heart by opening the windows of heaven and pouring out blessings.

Before you pray for something, ask yourself if your desire is a godly one. If it is, then wait patiently to see what God will do. Remember that when you trust Him with your life, everything will work out for the best.

Dear God, thank You for loving me enough to
choose what's best for my life instead of
spoiling me with what I want. Amen.

Know that wisdom is like this to your soul. If you find it, there will be a future, and your hope will not be cut off.
PROVERBS 24:14

DO YOU BELIEVE GOD HAS A SPECIFIC PLAN FOR YOUR LIFE?

Look at the man without blame. And watch the man who is right and good. For the man of peace will have much family to follow him.
PSALM 37:37

ARE YOU WORRIED ABOUT YOUR FUTURE?
WHY OR WHY NOT?

There is a special time for everything. There is a time for everything that happens under heaven.
ECCLESIASTES 3:1

IS IT POSSIBLE TO BE FULL OF PEACE WITH THE BAD
THINGS GOING ON IN THE WORLD TODAY?

The mind of a man plans his way,
but the Lord shows him what to do.
PROVERBS 16:9

HAVE YOU ASKED GOD TO SHOW
YOU HIS PLAN FOR YOUR LIFE?
IF NOT, TALK TO HIM RIGHT NOW.

The Lord Who bought you and saves you, the Holy One of Israel, says, "I am the Lord your God, Who teaches you to do well, Who leads you in the way you should go."
ISAIAH 48:17

DO YOU OFTEN STRUGGLE WITH WANTING YOUR WAY,
WHEN IT SEEMS GOD HAS OTHER PLANS?

The world and all its desires will pass away. But the man who obeys God and does what He wants done will live forever.
1 JOHN 2:17

WHAT DO YOU THINK THE FUTURE WILL BE LIKE IF YOU FOLLOW GOD'S LEAD?

There are many plans in a man's heart,
but it is the Lord's plan that will stand.
PROVERBS 19:21

DO YOU BELIEVE GOD IS IN CONTROL OF YOUR LIFE TODAY AND EVERY DAY? IF SO, HOW DOES THAT MAKE YOU FEEL?

But as for me, I will watch for the Lord. I will wait for the God Who saves me. My God will hear me.

MICAH 7:7

WHAT SCRIPTURES REMIND YOU
TO TRUST GOD WITH YOUR FUTURE?

The Holy Spirit is coming. He will lead you into all truth. He will not speak His Own words. He will speak what He hears. He will tell you of things to come.
JOHN 16:13

DO YOU BELIEVE THAT GOD HAS PLACED
BIG DREAMS IN YOUR HEART?

He stores up perfect wisdom for those who are right with Him. He is a safe-covering to those who are right in their walk.
PROVERBS 2:7

AS YOU THINK ABOUT THE FUTURE, DO YOU HAVE
"WHAT-IF" THOUGHTS THAT CAUSE YOU TO WORRY?
WHAT CAN YOU DO TO GET RID OF THE "WHAT-IFS"?

But they who wait upon the Lord will get new strength.
They will rise up with wings like eagles. They will run
and not get tired. They will walk and not become weak.
ISAIAH 40:31

WHAT IS A FAVORITE SCRIPTURE THAT REMINDS YOU TO GIVE YOUR WORRIES TO GOD?

Who is the man who fears the Lord? He will teach him in the way he should choose.
PSALM 25:12

HAVE YOU ASKED GOD TO HELP YOU MAKE
GOOD CHOICES THAT WILL AFFECT YOUR FUTURE?
IF YOU HAVEN'T, NOW IS A GREAT TIME
TO START THAT CONVERSATION WITH HIM.

Hope that is put off makes the heart sick,
but a desire that comes into being is a tree of life.
PROVERBS 13:12

WHAT DREAMS DO YOU HAVE FOR YOUR FUTURE?

Wisdom helps one to do well.
ECCLESIASTES 10:10

DO YOU SOMETIMES ALLOW YOUR PAST FAILURES
TO HOLD YOU BACK FROM TRYING NEW THINGS?

The fear of the Lord leads to life, and he who has it will sleep well, and will not be touched by sin.
PROVERBS 19:23

HOW DOES IT FEEL TO KNOW THAT GOD HOLDS YOUR FUTURE IN HIS HANDS?

*I am sure that God Who began the good
work in you will keep on working in you
until the day Jesus Christ comes again.*
PHILIPPIANS 1:6